Spirituality
and
Psychiatry
A Biblical Perspective

Ibrahim Youssef, PH.D.

www.mustardseedcounseling.co.uk

WORKBOOK PRESS LLC
187 E Warm Springs Rd,
Suite B285, Las Vegas, NV 89119, USA

Website: https://workbookpress.com/
Hotline: 1-888-818-4856
Email: admin@workbookpress.com

Ordering Information:
Quantity sales. Special discounts are available on quantity purchases by corporations, associations, and others. For details, contact the publisher at the address above.

ISBN-13:   978-1-953839-37-4 (Paperback Version)
                                   978-1-953839-38-1 (Digital Version)

REV. DATE: 08.01.2021

Dedication

To my wife Salwa and my daughter Joyce

CONTENTS

Preface

In 2009, the Royal College of Psychiatrists London UK, published an inflammatory book titled, "Spirituality and Psychiatry." The book was edited by 3 giants in the field of Psychiatry: Chris Cook, Andrew Powell and Andrew Sims. Each of the editors has served as a Chair of the Spirituality and Psychiatry Special Interest Group of the Royal College of Psychiatrists. It is striking to me to discover that in every time, they mention Christian faith, they are far from the biblical truth of the Scripture. Not only that but also, after each chapter, the book is ended   with tens of references, none of these includes the Bible.

What also make me sad , is when the book comes to discuss the Christian religion among the world most famous religions, the writers of this chapter: Mohamed Omar Salem and John Forskett, make an unforgivable theologian mistake by saying that the Lord Jesus was just a prophet lived in Palestine and was executed by the Romans around 30-33 CE, which is contrary to the Christian faith, that the Lord Jesus is God manifested Himself in the flesh. He sacrificed Himself on the Cross to redeem us from the penalty of sin which is death and to grant the believers in Him the eternal life. John 3:16 says, "For God so loved the world that He gave His only begotten Son (the Lord Jesus), that whoever believes in Him should not perish but have everlasting life."

This book is an invaluable resource for those Christians who are involved in mental illness as it covers most areas in psychiatry in a biblical perspective with extensive biblical references.

Ibrahim Youssef Ph.D
Dorchester
December 2020

---

1 Spirituality and Psychiatry, Chapter 12 written by Mohamed Salem and John Foskett, Royal College of Psychiatrists' publication, 2009. page 238

Chapter 1
Spirituality in the Bible

What is spirituality according to the Scripture? In Christian faith there are two kinds of spiritualities: The God's Spirit (the Holy Spirit) with His angels against the demonic spirits of Satan (the devil) with the evil spirits.

First, the Holy Spirit is the Spirit of God. John 4:24 records what the Lord Jesus says, *"God is Spirit and those who worship Him must worship in spirit and truth."* The Holy Spirit, the Spirit of God, who dwells in the believers, ties one to God and to the other believers (the church). In Genesis 2 verse 7, *"And the Lord God formed man of the dust of the ground., and breathed into his nostrils the breath of life; and man became a living being."* We can see that the body (of Adam) was formed with the brain (nostrils in head) from dust. Then God breathed in Adam's nostrils (Spirit/ soul) and he was created as a full man: body, soul/spirit and mind. God is eternal, so His breath is eternal. The man was created to be dependent on God. However, Adam and Eve (created from Adam) decided to be separated from Him and to be independent. As the result of the Fall, Adam and Eve with the all follow humankind and the earth had become belong to the kingdom of the prince of air, Satan. Until the Lord Jesus (the second Adam) came to defeat Satan (Hebrew says in 1 :2 *"has in these last days God has spoken to us by His Son, whom He has appointed heir of all things, through whom also He made the worlds).* He defeated Satan in the battle of the Cross and restore the relationship with man that was broken by the sin of the first Adam.

To understand, how does the Holy Spirit work in the World? Samuel Jardine[1] quotes John 16:8, when the Lord Jesus says that, *"And when He (the Holy Spirit) has come, He will convince the World of sin, and of righteousness, and of judgement."* Jardine explains this verse by saying that the conviction of sin is the refusal of Christ as the Saviour; of righteousness, that Christ is the only sinless person who carried our sins when He died for us on the Cross and lastly of judgement of the ruler of the World, Satan, who was already been defeated and judged, and is waiting to be executed and those who follow him will share his doom.

However, the Holy Spirit works in the believers in a different way, The Holy Spirit is given to all new believers immediately and unconditionally. 1 Corinthians 6:19, the Apostle Paul tells the believers of Corinth, *"Or do you know that your body is the temple of the Holy Spirit who is in you, whom you have from God, and you are not your own?"* The salvation here has referred to its origin of the loving Father; it has its basis in the redemptive work of the Son, as well as, it has its eternal security and present enjoyment in the presence of the Holy Spirit. The Holy Spirit is the *Paraklete* , the Greek word that can be translated as counsellor encourager, advocate or as a helper in time of trouble.

<u>Second</u>, Satan was created by God. He was a head angel worshiping God in His throne of Heaven. However, because of his sin of pride, he fell from heaven to earth taking with him third of evil angels. Isiah 14:12-15

---

1 Samuel Jardine, *The Person and the Work of the Holy Spirit.* (Stanton Drew, Bristol: Seed Publication, 2010) pp 27-33

explains his tragic fall, by saying *"How you are fallen from heaven, O Lucifer[2], son of the morning! How you are cut down to the ground. You who weakened the nations! For you have said in your heart: I will ascend into heaven, I will exalt my throne above the stars of God; I will also sit on the mount of the congregation. On the farthest sides of the north; I will ascend above the heights of the clouds; I will be like the Highest. Yet you shall be brought down to sheol, to the lowest depths of the Pit.*

So, according to above verses and to most of the bible scholars: it happened perhaps some millions or billions of years ago or so, Satan fell down to earth and made it "without form and void and darkness was on the face of the deep. And the Spirit of God was hovering over the face of the waters." (Genesis 1:2).

However, after the creation and because of the Fall of Adam and Eve, Satan has become the ruler of the earth and the prince of the air. The earth has become the kingdom of Satan. Then Christ came into this world and defeated him on the battle of the Cross as above. In Genesis 3:15, God said to the serpent (Satan), *"I will put enmity between you and the woman (Virgen Mary) and between your seed and her seed (refers to the Lord Jesus). He shall bruise (in some translations crush) your head. And you shall bruise His heel (refers to the Cross)."*

The Devil works through the unbelievers as the Apostle Paul says to the believers of Ephesus in Ephesians 2:2: *"in which you once walked (in sins) according to the course of this World, according to the prince of the power of the air, the spirit who now works in the sons of disobedience."*

---

2 Literally Day Star

The **Spiritual warfare**:

In Ephesians 6 :12, the Apostle Paul warns us that Satan and his demonic angels are well organised kingdom as "we are not wrestling against flesh and blood but against principalities, against powers , against the rulers of the darkness of this age, against spiritual hosts of wickedness in the heavenly places." Then he talks about the spiritual warfare and the believers should wear the spiritual armour to win this warfare battle. So, in Ephesians 6:13-18, the Apostle Paul says, *"therefore take up the whole armour of God that you may be able to withstand in the evil day. And having done all, to stand. Stand therefore having girded your waist with truth, having put on the breastplate of righteousness and having shod your feet with the preparation of the gospel of peace; above all, taking the shield of faith, with which you will be able to quench all the fiery darts of the wicked one. And take the helmet of salvation, and the sword of the Spirit, which is the word of God; praying always with all prayer and supplication in the Spirit, being watchful to this end with all perseverance and supplications for all saints."* However, Satan was defeated on the battle of the Cross and in Christ *"yet in all these things we are more than conquerors through Him who loved us"* (Romans 8:37).

In this context, R.T. Kandell(2007)[3] points out that Satan is real (despite the claim of secular psychologists and psychiatrists that he is not). However we need to believe that God put him under control, so he cannot harm the believers unless God allows him to do that for a reason. Satan's main tactic is to accuse the believers of their sins that they did in the past before salvation. He is the great accuser. In revelation 12:10, the Apostle

---

3 R.T Kendall, *"Totally Forgiving Ourselves"* Hodder & Stoughton Publication 2007 pp132-148

John says, *"Then I heard a loud voice saying in heaven, our God and the power of His Christ have come, **the accuser** of our brethren, who accused them before our God day and night has been cast down."*

Besides wearing the armour of God above, Kendall explains the 3 Rs to win this warfare battle. We need to: Recognise, Refuse, and Resist. In James 4: 7 says." *Therefore, submit to God. Resist the devil and he will flee from you."* If he accuses us about our past, we need to remind him about his doom future. We defeat him by believing in the blood of the Lamb. The blood of the Lord Jesus ,that He shed for us on the Cross, wipes away all our sins. Revelation 12:11 continues to say, *"And they overcome him((Satan) by the blood of the Lamb and by the word of their testimony."*

Chapter 2

Psychosis

Susan Mitchell and Glenn Roberts say at the start of their chapter of psychosis in "Spirituality and Psychiatry" that, "both spirituality and psychosis share a sense of mystery and each is notoriously difficult to define."[4] This statement is not true for the believers of the Bible. Spirituality as explained above, is not a mystery. Besides, believers who are filled with the Holy Spirit can discern the S/spirits, where "S" in the upper case refers to the Holy Spirit the Spirit of God, while "s" in the lower case refers to demonic spirits[5]. What is more, for some believers, they have the gift of casting out the demonic spirits.[6]

In the Old Testament, we do not read about prophets who could cast out demonic spirits. Cast out demons was done only by the Lord Jesus when He was on earth (Mt 4:24,9:32,12:22). What is more, the Lord Jesus gave this power to his disciples and before his ascent to heaven, He gave this power also to the believers in Him. In Mark 16:17, the Lord Jesus says, *"And these signs will follow those who believe: in My name they will cast out demons; they will speak with new tongues."*

So, for the Christian believers, there is no confusion about the spirituality. With the gift of discerning S/spirits, they can differentiate between who is that from God (the Holy Spirit) and who is that from Satan (demonic).

But what about psychosis?

Psychosis is a cluster of symptoms in patients with schizophrenic disorders and other severe psychiatric disorders like severe depression and manic disorders.

DSM-IV-TR (American Psychiatric Association, 2000)[7] defines psychosis that the person should have two or more of the followings, each present for at least 1-month period or less if successfully treated:

1. Delusions
2. Hallucinations
3. Disorganised speech
4. Grossly disorganised or catatonic behaviour
5. Negative symptoms: affective flattening, alogia or avolition

Note: Only one of the above is required if delusions are bizarre or hallucinations of commentary voices or two or more voices conversing with each other.

The delusions and hallucination are usually accompanied of fear, generated both by the experience and/or because the person is afraid, he or she may not be believed if they share their experience with others. Madness can appear as a perplexing constellation of odd experience, perceptions and beliefs.

The confusion between the religious or faith-beliefs from delusions of psychosis was back to Freud[8] (1927) who have regarded religious beliefs as delusions, on the basis that religion is inherently fabricated and therefore

7 DSM-IV-TR, American Psychiatric Association, Arlington, VA (2000).
8 Freud. S. (1927) The future of an illusion. In The complete works of Sigmoid Freud (eds) Strachery & A Freud). Hogarth Press

beliefs associated with it are also false-according to him. However, for Christians, they have the Bible, the word of God that differentiates easily between the two. The Christian believers believe in 2 Timothy 1:7, *"For God has not given us a spirit of fear(other translations, failure), but of power, and of love, and of a sound mind(other translations, self-control)."* If in doubt the treating psychiatrist could consult a priest or pastor, who have knowledge and experience in this field.

The Lord Jesus differentiates between psychosis as mental illness (in Psalm 103:3 says *"Bless the Lord, O my soul ----who heals all your diseases,"* to include mental illness) and the demonic spirits that He delivered the sufferers from.

Examples of casting out demons are as follows:

1. Mathew 8: 28-34: (also in Mark 5:1-20, here is one not two, perhaps mentioned the one who was the most suffered, also in Luke 8:22-29, here also only one man is mentioned for the same reason in Mark), the Lord Jesus casted out demons from two persons who had severe disturbed behaviour(he wore no clothes and did not live in a house but in tombs) . The demons could not withstand the presence of God. In verses 8:30-32, the demons begged the Lord, *"Now a good way of them, there was a herd of many swine feeding. So, the demons begged Him saying, If You cast us out, permit us to go away into the herd of swine. And He (the Lord) said to them, "Go." So, when they had come out , they went into the herd of swine. And suddenly the whole herd of swine ran violently down the steep place into the sea and perished in the water."* So, it is clearly Demon's possession not mental illness as the latter is not transmitted from

humans to pigs.

2. Mathew 17:14-21: (also in Mark 9:14-29, also in Luke 9:27-43) when the Lord Jesus casted out demons from a boy. Here the demons made this boy had what is seemed to be epileptic fits which made him cry in a loud voice and throw himself into fire when he had these attacks. His father brought him to the Lord's disciples who could not cast out the demons. It seemed the demons had a strong hold on the boy. So, the Lord told the disciples that this kind of demons can only be delivered from the boy by prayers and fasting.

3. Mark 1:21-28: Here we find a religious Jewish man who was worshiping God in the synagogue. He was normal in appearance. However, the demon in him could not withstand the presence of God in flesh, so the demon cried out pleading from the Lord not destroy him. Here the Lord ordered the demon to shut up even the demon was talking of the right thing (that the Lord Jesus is the Holy One of God) because the Lord does not accept testimony from demons. Then the Lord rebuked the demon to get out from the man, so he did. Here also we notice that the Jews were amazed as they knew from the Old Testament that only God can cast out demons.

4. Luke 13:10-17: Here the Lord casted out a demon of infirmity that caused a woman to suffer from physical problem of severe Kyphosis (severe bending of the spine). What we notice here is that the woman was a religious Jewish worshiping God in the synagogue. The behaviour was normal. But the Lord Jesus who discerns the spirits, knew that the woman's back bending posture was caused by a demon of infirmity. So, the Lord rebuked that spirit to get out

from the woman, so the women back had straightened. Also, from this incident we learn that demons have specialities

In summary, the Christians who are born-again in Water (the word of God) and the Spirit (the Holy Spirit) as in John 3, has two main privileges in this context:

1. Safeguard against psychosis: They should pray for the sound mind according to 2 Timothy 1:7.

2. Safeguard against demons: when they wear the full armour of God in Ephesians 6 and resist the devil when he attacks them in James 4:7. So The devil would not touch them; according to 1 John 5:18 , *"we know that whoever is born of God does not sin (or continue in sinning), but he who has been born of God keeps himself and the wicked one (the devil) does not touch him (or her)."*

Practical Application

Case study 2.1[9]

Alan, a friendless man living in poverty, believed himself to be an unemployed Messiah and was waiting to be called forward in the second coming. He attended church each week, staying near the alter so as to receive the genuflections of communicants as worship. He believed that the many tourists who visited his town in the summer were his pilgrims.

Comments:

This a straight forward case of schizophrenia with bizarre delusions, loss

---

9 Chris Cook et all. Spiritualty and psychiatry. Royal College of Psychiatrists London UK publications (2010) page 42

of insight and poor function (unemployed, has no friends). However, he needs to sit with the priest or pastor of that church he attends to explain to him the Christian faith and what is meant by the second coming of Messiah according to the Scripture. The fixed bizarre delusions like this, are difficult to be challenged , so he needs to continue on antipsychotic for his psychotic illness.

Case Study 2.2[10]

James, a middle-aged man, had a strong sense of religious vocation and liked to attend mass each day, often acting as acolyte. He believed that divine healing was more important than medication and psychotherapy, which he felt were only half the story. Yet he regularly relapsed severely into a catatonic state either when medication was reduced or if he became an informal patient and stopped taking medication on his own initiative. During relapse his religious beliefs took on an intense delusional quality.

Comments:

This is a frequent presentation of a psychotic patient who refuses to take medication or attends psychotherapy, believing that he is healed by God and no need for such things. As above, he needs to sit with the pastor or priest of his church he attends, to explain to him that God is the healer who heals through medication and he needs to continue on it to prevent relapse of his illness. Fortunately, he has partial insight into his illness so the delusional beliefs could be softened with medication and/or psychotherapy.

---

10 Same reference above page 52.

Chapter 3

Suicide

Cherrie Coghlan and Imran Ali (2009)[11], defines Spirituality as that it is dealing with life, death and meaning of life. For suicide could happen when there is distortion in these concepts. Suicide in the past was legally regarded as a murder and the attempted suicide was regarded as attempted murder. But things have changed, as now it is seen as an issue for the helping professions rather than the law. The religious attitudes were also shifted to one of compassion for the deceased and support of the bereaved-according to Coghlan and Ali.

Biblical perspective for the issue of suicide:

Besides it is one of the Ten Commandments *"You shall not murder"* in Exodus 20:13, Christian believers believe that our bodies are not of our-own in three respects: first, we are created by God as we do not create ourselves, Second, Jesus Christ bought us and delivered us from the Kingdom of Satan to the Kingdom of God. He paid the price which is His precious blood that was shed for us on the Cross. We took salvation by grace not by our deeds. In John 3:16, the Lord Jesus says, *"For God so loved the world that He gave His only begotten Son, that whoever believes in Him should not perish but have everlasting life." Third, our bodies are temples of the Holy Spirit. Apostle Paul says in 1 Corinthians 6:19, "Or do you know that your body is the temple of the Holy Spirit who is in you, whom you have from God and you are not your own,"*

But even so, Coghlan and Ali say that Christian faith neither praises nor condemns the act of suicide[12], that show their ignorance of the biblical truth. They code examples of king Saul who killed himself because of humiliation after he was defeated in a battle (1 Samuel 31:1-4) also Judas Iscariot's death who killed himself by hanging because of the severe guilt that he felt after he betrayed his Master, the Lord Jesus (Mathew 27:3-5).

But for Samson the matter is different. Samson was consecrated to live for God and was appointed by Him to serve as a Judge of the Israelites. However, he had no self-control over the temptation of lust for a woman called Delilah, who cut his hair (sign of consecration so he was separated from God, the source of power). As the result he fell captive by the enemy who plugged his eyes and put him in prison. He was then dragged to the feast of his enemy's gods. However, he prayed to God, *"Then Samson called to the Lord, saying "O Lord God, remember me, I pray! Strengthen me, I pray just this once, O God that I may with one blow take vengeance on the Philistines for my two eyes!"* (Judges 16 :28). He then pushed the two pillars of the temple of the enemy causing the building to collapse, killing himself and his captors. The Bible records that he prayed twice in this occasion most likely he repented his sins and pleaded for God's mercy. God answered him and allowed this to happen. So, we cannot say that he committed suicide. Also, it is not a homicide either because that was the fair judgment of God on the enemy for their sins, they committed against Him (they worshiped other gods also they murdered God's people). Besides their barbaric act of plugging Samson's eyes. To confirm that his death is neither suicide nor homicide, the Holy Spirit records Samson among the list of the giants of faith in Hebrews 11 verse 32, *"And what more shall I say? For the time would*

---

12 The same reference above page 66.

fail me to tell of Gideon and Barak and Samson and Jephthah, also of David and Samuel and the prophets."

<u>Spiritual issues in the clinical management of people with suicidal thoughts</u>

Coghlan and Ali records in their chapter of suicide that there is a professional and social expectation that psychiatrists have a duty to prevent suicide, which reflects moral and religious views about the wrongness of suicide.

For Christian believers, the matter is different, suicide is regarded sin. Is it unforgivable sin? It is left to God to judge. But generally, it is as a murder of life which is a gift from God the creator as mentioned above. I believe that every Christian believer who attempts suicide should be seen by a pastor or a priest of the church. But the matter is complicated not as it looks. On one hand, the professions fear wrongly that the minister of the church could promote suicide. On the other hand, the priest or pastor may feel that if they see an individual who attempts suicide, he or she might commit suicide after been seen, so the church then would get the blame.

But there is exception, patients with severe depression or schizophrenia like illness may have distorted religious beliefs even they are strong believers. So, such patients Should adequately be treated before been seen by church ministers.

Case study 3.1[13]

Mike is a married Christian man in his late 50s. His wife went for a religious festive and been away from home when she had an affair with another man.

---

13 Real-life case scenario but the names and location been changed for confidentiality.

His wife confessed to him about the affair and the couple decided to move on with their marriage as they have two sons. During a Christmas dinner, Mike re-opened the subject with his wife blaming her that she still loves that man not him. He then slapped his wife on her face. His wife called the police and Mike was admitted to psychiatric ward as he related his behaviour to depression that he suffered. During his admission, he heard that his wife is dating that man whom she had an affair with. Mike asked to go out from the ward which was granted as the risk for suicide considered low. He went out and hanged himself.

Comments:

This is a tragic real-life case of Christian couple who have distorted religious beliefs about the message of the Gospel which calls for repentance and forgiveness of God based on the grace Also, they had distorted meaning and the goal of marriage which is ordained by God to live in intimacy and purity of the Spirit. Biblical marriage counselling could save lives. The case also shows how the devil destroys lives as he has been the murderer from the beginning. The Lord Jesus says about the devil in John 8:44, to the pharisees who wanted to kill Him , *"You are of your father the devil, and the desires of your father you want to do. He was a murderer from the beginning, and does not stand in the truth, because there is no truth in him, when he speaks a lie, he speaks from his own resources, for he is a liar and the father of it."*

Case Study 3.2[14]

Mr X is a successful business man. He has an affair with one of his female

---

14 Real-life case scenario. The name is kept anonymous for confidentiality.

workers. So, his wife left him with two young children. His business is crumbled and is admitted to the psychiatric ward with depression and suicidal ideation. He told the psychiatrist that his brother and his father committed suicide and now it is his turn. Because he has no clinical depression, and apart from ruminating suicidal thoughts, the risk of suicide is considered low. So, he is discharged to be followed up by the community team. A couple of weeks later he commits suicide.

Comments:

This is a preventable suicide case. There is a demonic suicidal curse in the family as the patient's brother and father committed suicide and the patient says it is his turn. The case is preventable in the way that if he is committed Christian, or been evangelised if not, he could be seen by a pastor or priest, who would advise him to rebuke the demons of death in the family. James 4:7 says, *"Therefore submit to God. Resist the devil and he will flee from you."* With Christ there is always hope for reconciliation of marriage also there is hope that the business will flourish again.

Chapter 4

Depression

Depression is the most common psychiatric disorder. For us as Christians, we believe that all Christians can experience fear, upset, and depression at some stages of their lives. Being a Christian does not prevent us or our loved ones from experience depression. Also, we believe that we do not see anxiety and depression as always being the result of sin, neither do we believe that mental illness problems are the result of lack of faith.

DSM-IV-TR (2000)[15] defines Depression as five (or more) of the following symptoms are present during the same two weeks period and represent a change from previous functioning and at least one of the symptoms is either (1) depressed mood or (2) loss of interest or pleasure.

1. Depressed mood
2. Loss of interest or pleasure
3. Significant wight loss or weight gain
4. Insomnia or hypersomnia
5. Psychomotor agitation or retardation
6. Fatigue or loss of energy
7. Feelings worthless
8. Lack of concentration

---

15 Diagnostic criteria from DSM-IV-TR, American Psychiatric Association Arlington VA (2000).pages 168-169.

9. Suicidal ideation.

The above is not related directly to physical illness or substance misuse.

We can look at Anxiety and Depression as a spectrum, with pure anxiety and pure depression at opposite ends. But mixing together in the middle. In bipolar illness both depression and hypomania or mania are present in alternation each at a time.

Biblical perspective of depression and anxiety:

God created Adam and Eve to live in harmony with each other and to have a dependant relationship on God. However, as the result of the Fall when they sinned to God as they wanted to be separated for Him when they ate from the tree that God forbidden them to eat from, their eyes were opened and they knew the good from the evil as they then appreciated that they were naked. As the result they were expelled from the Garden of Eden. Genesis three goes on to describe how through choice, mankind sinned and damaged previously close relationship with God, with fellow human beings and with the environment. The consequences of this are that we now live in a world where life can be painful and difficult. We see this in the moral, physical, economic and spiritual problems that occur around us and that sometimes result in damage and suffering.

However, there is hope, even before the creation, God knew about the Fall of the mankind and prepared a solution which He declared in Genesis 3:15 when God said to the Serpent (Satan) *"And I will put enmity between you and the woman, And between your seed and her seed (Jesus Christ who was born from the Virgin Mary) , He shall bruise (some translations crush) your head, and you shall bruise His heel (when the Lord died on the Cross to redeem us, then in the 3rd day, He rose from the grave),"*

One consequence of the Fall is that we are brought up in a world that has been damaged and our experience of being brought up is likely has damaged us in at least some ways. Whatever our experiences, it is likely that as we grew up, we learned a range of helpful and unhelpful rules about how we see and judge ourselves, other people and the world around us. It is in childhood that these central ways of seeing things are first learned from our relationship with important people such as parents, brothers or sisters. In these relationships we should receive love, consistency and support but sometimes the opposite occurs- rejection and inconsistency- and this can undermine us as we grow up. These central ways of seeing things are called *core beliefs.*

These core beliefs can be a mixture of negative and positive ones. for example, being good and successful at work but failure in marriage and relationships. Most of the time, we try to suppress or dismiss the negative ones, but at the time of distress, anxiety and depression, not only we notice the negative core beliefs, but also such thoughts occur more frequently.

R.T. Kendall[16]talks about guilt and pseudo guilt. On one hand, guilt when we commit true sins and feel guilty about that as all sins are committed against God as Psalm 51:4 declares, *"against You, You only have I sinned. And done this evil in Your sight-"* For the believers, the Holy Spirit reminds us with these sinful acts and directs us to repentance and reconciliation of the relationship with God whom we sinned against Him. 1 John 1:9 says, *"If we confess our sins, He is faithful and just will forgive our sins and purify us from all unrighteousness."* And there is now no condemnation for those

---

16 R.T Kendall, *Totally Forgiving Ourselves,* (London. UK, Hodder & Stoughton: 2007).

who are in Christ Jesus." (Romans 8:1). Again, it is the work of the Holy Spirit (who dwells in the believers) to convict us when we sin and direct us to repentance and forgiveness by God whom we sin against. For the unbelievers because they do not have the Holy Spirit, they would sin but do not recognise that and continue in sinning as they regard that as normal.

On the other hand, pseudo guilt can bother both believers and unbelievers. It is when we do things and later on, we recognise that we made wrong choices because of the bad judgment, so we regret and feel bad of ourselves.

In depression both guilt and pseudo guilt are intensified and come up more frequently. For guilt, the believers, we should forgive ourselves as God forgave us as above. For pseudo guilt, we also need not to continue of condemning ourselves but learning from our mistakes. The pseudo-guilt would become sin if we continue to feel like this. So, we need to repent asking for God's forgiveness as we believe that, *"And we know that all things work together for good to those who love God, to those who are called according to His purpose."* (Romans 8:28).

The role of the devil in depression is to make believers feel more guilt about sins they committed in the past. No wonder he is called the great accuser. Our weapon is to resist him with the word of God, the sword of the Spirit as the Apostle Paul says in Ephesians 6:17. If devil reminds us with our sins in the past, we need to remind him with his doomed future. Our sins in the past have been covered and been forgiven by the blood of the Lamb, Jesus Christ's blood that was shed for us on the Cross. Revelation 12:11 says, *"And they overcame him (the devil, Satan) by the blood of the Lamb and by the word of their testimony."* By believing and saying to ourselves that the blood of the Lamb wipes away all our sins as long as we repent and believe in the blood of Jesus.

Kendall summarises his book as follows[17]:

The purpose of this book could be summarized right here. If you and I can make the distinction in our minds between guilt- and deal with it - and pseudo guilt and not governed by it, we are on our way to inner peace and freedom.

Added to the above, "Chris Williams 2002" points out that part of the Christian maturity is to be able to begin to see ourselves as God sees us – as someone who is loved by Him in spite of areas, we all have in our lives that continue to be wrong.

Case Study 4.1

This case study is from the Old Testament in 1 Kings 19:1-8

And Ahab told Jezebel all that Elijah has done, also how he had executed all the prophets of Baal with the sword. Then Jezebel sent a messenger to Elijah, saying, "So let the gods do to me and more also, if I do not make your life as the life of one of them by tomorrow about this time." And when he(Elijah) saw that (other translations, he was afraid) he arose and ran for his life and went to Beesheba, which belongs to Judah and left his servant there. But he himself went a day's journey into the wildness and came and sat down under a broom tree. And he prayed that he might die and said, "It is enough! Now Lord take my life, for I am no better than my fathers." Then as he lay and slept under a broom tree, suddenly an angel touched him, and said to him, "Arise and eat." Then he looked and there by his head was a cake baked on coals and a jar of water. So, he ate and drank and lay down again. And the angel of the Lord came back the

---

17 The same reference above page 89.

second time, and touched him and said arise and eat, because the journey is too great
for you." So, he arose and ate and drank; and he went in the strength of that food
forty days and forty nights as far as Horeb, the mountain of God (mount Sinai).

Comments

This is a beautiful case scenario from the Bible about the man of God, the prophet Elijah who suffered depression. He had five symptoms of depression and anxiety and according DSM-IV-TR, we can easily diagnose his case as major depressive disorder: low mood, loss of interest, fatigue, hypersomnia and suicidal ideation. Besides, he had anxiety feared the evil woman Jezebel would kill him.

The causes of that might be exhaustion after he killed 450 prophets of Ball the day before and he was afraid that he would be killed by the woman Jezebel so he preferred to die by God better than to die by a woman. He was touched by the angel and totally healed from his depression by God who provided him with food (for us the word of God in the Scripture) and jar of water (for us the filling of the Holy Spirit). We note here that Elijah slept again but God was persistent as the angel arose him again to eat and to drink. That meal and drink gave him strength for forty days and forty nights while he was walking in the desert to Horeb , the mountain of God (mount Sinai) where God appeared to him to give him tasks to do.

Case Study 4.2

Melena is a 55-year-old woman suffers from depressive disorder. She is married and has two grown up children who left home. She lives with her husband of 35 years of marriage. No causes for depression as her family is supportive. Although she stopped working as a secretary because of her depression, she has no financial problems. She is Christian. beside her antidepressants, she is also receiving CBT (Cognitive Behaviour Therapy) from a secular psychologist. She confesses to her pastor that before her marriage, she had a physical relationship with a man. Although it is normal in western society a boyfriend could leave his girlfriend or vice versa, she ,as a new convert, has great problem in dealing with guilt because of that. So, she says her faith instead of being a help becomes a hindrance.

Comments

Melena is a believer, new-born Christian. Ephesians 2:8 says, *"For by grace you have been saved through faith, and that not of yourselves; it is a gift of God."* So, she is saved by grace and she has the Holy Spirit. One of the jobs of the Holy Spirit is the conviction of sin. She recognizes now what she did before marriage was sin. So, she needs to repent her sin asking for God's forgiveness. 1 John 1:9 says, *"if we confess our sins, He (the Lord) is faithful and just to forgive us our sins and to cleanse us from all unrighteousness."* However, the devil (Satan) continues in condemning her by reminding her of her past, taking advantage of her depression to get things worse difficult to be treated by antidepressants and CBT. The answer is she needs to see a biblical counsellor to have a brief counselling. Basically, to highlight the word of God to her and how to apply the Scripture to resist the devil. Satan is the great accuser. She could use the 3 Rs technique mentioned above (Recognize, Refuse and Resist). Then she will enjoy peace in the midst of her suffering of depression.

Case study 4.3

Alice is 35-year-old Christian woman suffers from clinical depression.

She has just finished her 12th session provided by a professional biblical counsellor with no improvement. She met her friend, Jane who told her about the antidepressant Prozac that can be prescribed by her General Practitioner. however, Alice is reluctant to do that as she believes that God is the healer and He can heal her without medication.

Comments

This is a common mistake that Christians sometimes insist on God to heal them from depression without medication. Although that can be true, God also can heal with the prescribed medication. My advice is to pray that God will direct her GP to prescribe antidepressant which is suitable for her case. The antidepressants should be taken for at least 6 months and not to stop without advice of her doctor.

Chapter 5
Psychotherapy

Historically, madness was related to demons and evil spirits (Satan and his fallen angels). So, much of the care of mental ill patients had been provided within a spiritual or religious context (Sim et al 2009)[18].Not until the beginning of the 20th century, some definition of mental illness and the separation from religion had been established.

The secular psychotherapy and Christian models in a chronological order are summarized as follows:

1. Sigmoid Freud- psychoanalysis (1856-1939): he was affected by Darwen's theory of evolution. So, the man is animal -according to Freud- driven by sex and violence. The role of the counsellor or psychologist is to adjust his behaviour to be socially acceptable. Psychoanalysis model is still in use, but it has a disadvantage of being long and exhausting (the psychologist takes extensive childhood experiences with analysis).

2. Skinner-behaviour therapy (1904-1990): appeared at the time of the communism. The man is moulded by environment. So, the man is Zero-according to skinner. The role of the psychologist is to adjust the environment for the sake of the man (for example by

---

18 Andrew Sims and Christopher C H. Cook , Spirituality in Psychiatry chapter 1 *in Spirituality and Psychiatry* (Royal College of Psychiatrist publication, London 2009)page 1.

reward and punishment). The model is still in use for clients with learning disabilities and children.

3. Carl Rogers- humanism theory (1920-1987) man is full of potentials created by God who is no longer involved in His creation- according to Rogers. The role of the psychologists is to discover the client's potentials to encourage him to live up to his potentials. The humanism model was the most popular model before CBT model which was developed in the early 1970s, below.

4. Modern Cognitive Behaviour Therapy (CBT)in1970s: change the thinking (cognition) leads to change in feeling and behaviour. The role of the psychologist is to change the negative thoughts to positive ones or change the client's perception of a problem or situation, to be followed by change of his/her reaction and feeling. It is the most popularly used model. The religion (God) is present but irrelevant.

5. Jay Adams: Nouthetic counselling in 1970, when he published his first book, Competent to Counsel CtC. It is based on the confrontation of sin as the basis of change. It is pure biblical counselling developed by Adams to oppose the humanistic theory of Rogers . Adams blames Rogers for the decline of the moral values of the Americans.

6. Larry Crabb (1970s) integration of secular psychology with biblical counselling. This model was developed by Crabb as a reaction to the Nouthetic counselling of Adams.

7. Mindfulness therapy (1990s-2000s) From Buddhists' practice of meditation. As below.

8. Ibrahim Youssef (2016): pure biblical counselling based on the fruit and the charismatic gifts of the Holy Spirit.

Mindfulness

It is based on Buddhism's practice of meditation. All things are impermanence. The origin of suffering is in the attachment to things that are impermanent. The cessation of suffering is by the eradication of such things which result in the healing of the soul. It is used for chronic depression and anxiety, and psychosis. It is practised in groups where intrapersonal and interpersonal meditate on one issue at a time of -now and then- during closure of the eyes. It has attracted more and more interest in psychiatric practice as it connects psychiatry with spirituality and it is allowed in NHS secular settings.

For Christian meditation, it attracts interest of Christian believers but unless they meditate on the Scripture with the guide of the Holy Spirit, it can be dangerous as *the heart (the mind) is deceitful above all things, and desperately wicked; who can know it?*" (Jeremiah 17:9). That is why we need the gift of the Holy Spirit of "discerning the S/spirits." (1 Corinthians 12:10).

Case Study 5.1

Steve is 73-year-old man was admitted to the psychiatric ward. He went for his fourth session of CBT and confessed to the psychologist that he wanted to kill himself, so he was referred for admission. When he was seen by the psychiatrist, he told her that his late parents owned a farm and he was the only child of his parents. His parents abused him physically and emotionally. They treated him like a farm-animal. They forced him to work in the farm long hours and ignored his education. He managed to leave them to work as a cheap labour in a nearby farm for 25 years. His parents hired a stranger to work in the farm. Steve heard that his parents died and the stranger possessed the farm and did not give him any inheritance. Steve then managed to work as a carrier at the Royal mail, where he worked for another 25 years. He soaked himself in work trying to forget his past. At the age 68, he was forced to retire. He then moved to a retirement bedsit in a nearby town looking for a new start and to forget the painful past. He attended a church there where he was visited by the pastor of that church for 5 times for pastoral counselling. He did not get better and now he is feeling angry towards God because He allowed him to suffer all his years. He is taking antidepressants beside the CBT with no improvement.

Comments

It is obvious that this man's problem is spiritual. He was abused by his parents emotionally and physically (sexual abuse?). He was like a cow for them in his family farm. Then the parents left him to go to work in the nearby farm then they hired a stranger who possessed the farm after their death. So evil spirit worked in the family. After 50 plus years this man's spiritual problem float on the surface with deep negative emotions of mixture of anger, resentment and despair as he cannot change his past. After he was seen by a pastor, these negative emotions were directed towards God as he believes that He is responsible for his misery. Because the problem is spiritual the management should be spiritual.

This case can be managed by my spiritual model, the Mustard Seed Model[19] as follows:

---

19 This management is also recorded with modification from my book, *"The Mustard Seed Counseling,"* Authorhouse publication (2020). pp 84-88.

Early stage of justification:

1. Step one: salvation, the counsellor explains to Steve that when a new convert is born-again Christian, the Holy Spirit dwells in him (the metaphor of Mustard Seed). If Steve does not, he needs to pray the sinner's prayer and accepts the Lord Jesus as his Saviour. Repentance is part of the package of salvation. He has to repent his sin of unforgiveness towards his late parents. Repentance represents a fundamental change in thinking towards God. God is not responsible for his past misery. God did not create evil. The evil entered the world as the result of the sin of Adam and Eve. Sin distorts family relationship. For example, shortly after the Fall, Cain killed his brother Abel. Genesis 4:8, *"Now Cain talked with Abel his brother; and it came to pass, when they went in the field, that Cain rose up against Abel his brother and killed him."*

2. Step two: Die to the world, flesh and the devil. As the result of salvation, he is now a new creation in Christ. 2 Corinthians 5:17 says, *"therefore if anyone in Christ, he is a new creation; old things have passed away; behold, all things have become new."*

Middle stage of sanctification:

3. Step three: faith *pistis* (the Mustard Seed) is the key to the other fruit of the Spirit, mentioned in Galatians 5:22-23, namely love, joy, peace, long sufferings, kindness, goodness, gentleness, and self-control. Steve should pursue or strive to get this fruit with all its items in cluster, empowered by the Holy Spirit who dwells in him as a new believer. It is difficult to change all the negative emotions like anger and resentment towards his late parents overnight. The

change is achieved by the relationship with God in praying, reading the word of God in the Bible, attending a local Bible-based church, and meeting new friends of other believers. Other things like play sports like golf or even regular walking.

4. Step four: faith *pistis* (the Mustard Seed) is the key to the other charismatic gifts of the Spirit: here the Mustard Seed of faith, *pistis* that is originally implanted in step one by the Holy Spirit in salvation , has grown to bring the fruit of the Spirit in step 3, grows further , to bring the other supernatural gifts of the Holy Spirit listed in 1 Corinthians 8-10 namely the word of wisdom, the word of knowledge, healings, miracles, prophecy, tongues, and interpretation of tongues. Of these charismatic gifts, Steve needs the healings most, the healing of his memory which is one of these gifts of the Holy Spirit. The counsellor should pray with him to get this gift. The best example in the Bible (apart from the Lord Jesus' forgiveness our sins), is Joseph. He suffered a lot from his brothers who were jealous of him and they wanted to kill him but instead they sold him as a slave. When Joseph became the second man of Egypt after Pharaoh, the Bible teaches us that he forgave and forgot what his brothers had done for him and when he had his first-born child son, he named him Manasseh, as he said, *"For God has made me forget all my toil and all my father's house."* (Genesis 41:51).

Final stage of glorification:

5. Step five: faith *pistis* (the Mustard Seed) pulls up the roots of the problem: this is marvellous. According to the Lord Jesus in Luke 17 verse 6, *"if you have faith as a mustard seed, you can say to this*

mulberry tree, be pulled up by the roots and be planted in the sea and it would obey you." So, all the negative emotions of this man: bitterness, resentment, hurt, anger, suicidal ideation and so forth, as the result of his long years of sufferings will vanish. He may remember what his parents had done for him, but that would no longer disturb his peace, quietness and the joy of having the relationship with the Lord.

6. Step six: serve the Lord: serving the Lord comes naturally as the result of the above steps. It is part of sowing and reaping the fruit and the gifts of the Holy Spirit. It should be part of this man's life, something to live for, to give him value and purpose of life.

Chapter 6

Substance Misuse

Substance misuse psychiatry is concerned with what happens when people use psychoactive substances in such a way that they cause harm to themselves and others.

According to DSM-IV-TR (2000)[20] it is a maladaptive pattern of substance use, leading to clinically significant impairment or distress as manifested by three (or more) of the following, occurring at any time in the same 12-month period:

1.Tolerance: increase the amount of substance to achieve a desired effect or diminished effect with continued use of the same amount of substance.

2. Withdrawal: the use of the same amount or related substance to relieve or avoid withdrawal symptoms

3. Amount taken in a larger amount or over a longer period than was intended.

4.Persistamt desire to cut down or control of substance use but unsuccessful

5.A great deal of time is spent in activities necessary to obtain the substance

6.given up or reduced important social, occupational or recreational activities

---

20 American psychiatric Association 2000. Arlington VA (2000).

7. Substance taken in spite of the physical or psychological problems and the concern of friends and family.

A disease model has become popular and this disease was understood, in one form or another, as a disease of the will caused by substance, for example alcohol misuse.

This disease model, in a modified form, was adopted in the 20th century by Alcoholic Anonymous (AA), and it was this organisation that has had particular influence over the perception of addiction as a spiritual problem in North America and Europe. Founded in Akron, Ohio by two alcoholics in 1935, it is based on a basic Christian and biblical foundation that the person who is addict needs more than human power to help him/her to overcome the addiction problem.

Historical perception of AA

After the organization was established in 1935 and after three years of trial and error in selecting a workable foundation of the new society, three groups emerged at Akron, New York and Cleveland. In April 1939, the new society managed to publish its new book with twelve steps and the rest of the book was devoted for thirty cases who recovered using the new steps. The society then expanded through the USA states thanks to the free advertisements given by magazines and newspapers. Clergy and doctors rallied to the new movement, giving their support and endorsement. Soon arose threatening questions regarding money, legality, personal relation etc. So, in 1949, AA published 12 traditions that gave the new society its present form, substance and unity. By 1999, AA is established in 159 countries and the recoveries have exceeded two million. The twelve steps module means more than sobriety for problem of alcohol but is a way to happy and effective living for many addicts and AA expands to include many other addictions like narcotics anonymous, sex addiction anonymous etc.

The Twelve Steps:[21]

1. We admitted we were powerless over alcohol that our lives have become unmanageable.

2. Came to believe that a Power greater than ourselves could restore us to sanity.

3. Made a decision to turn our will and our lives over to the care of God (as we understand him).

4. Made a searching and fearless inventory of ourselves

5. Admitted to God and to another human-being the exact nature of our wrongs

6. Were entirely ready to have God remove all these defects of characters

7. Humbly asked Him to remove shortcoming

8. Made a list of all persons we had harmed, and became willing to make amends to them all

9. Made direct amends to such people wherever possible except when to do so would injury them or others

10. Continue to take a personal inventory and when we were wrong promptly admitted it

11. Sought through prayer and meditation to improve our conscious contact with God ,as we understood him, praying only for

---

21 Alcoholic Anonymous World Service Inc 1999, *Twelve Steps and Twelve Traditions* New York (1999).

knowledge of his will for us and the power to carry that out.

12. Having had a spiritual awakening as the result of these steps, we tried to carry this message to alcoholics and to practice these principles in all our affairs.

Comments:

1. From biblical perspective, alcohol addiction is sin (AA uses disease model) as in Ephesians 5:18s says *"And do not be drunk with wine, in which is dissipation; but be filled with the Spirit."* Also, in Proverbs 23:20 says, *"Do not mix with winebibber. Or with gluttonous eaters of meat (other translations the drunkards destroy their bodies)."* So, although the AA has a Christian basis, it fails in this respect. As a sin, the addict needs to repent asking for God's forgiveness.

In this context, Chris Cook (2006)[22] agrees on the disease model by saying that for Christian theology, grace rather than sin is central and it is grace that (in non-theological language) the 12 steps programmes have also identified as to vital recovery from addiction.

However, his opinion is far from the scriptural truth as the grace has never been an excuse to sin. In Romans 6:1-3, the Apostle Paul teaches us that, *"What shall we say then? Shall we continue in sin that grace may abound? Certainly not! How shall we who died to sin live any longer in it. Or do you not know that as many of us as were baptised into Christ Jesus were baptized into His death?* Also, our bodies are temples of the Holy Spirit as the Apostle Paul says in 1

---

22 Cook, C.C, H, *Alcohol Addiction and Christian Ethics.* Cambridge University Press(2006) page 146

Corinthians 6:19, *"or do you not know that your body is the temple of the Holy Spirit who is in you, whom you have from God and you are not your own?"*

Other alternative biblical models like "The Nouthetic" model of Jay Adams where the confrontation of sin is the basis of change or "The Mustard Seed Counselling" of Ibrahim Youssef where the Holy Spirit's fruit and His charismatic gifts are the basis of change can be used instead.

2. AA 12 steps acknowledges God *"as we understand"* which is a vague statement to suit other religions or even atheists who need to believe in the group's power! But it is not for us as Christians as we believe in God who manifested Himself in the Lord Jesus as in Hebrew 1:1-2, *" God, who at various times and in various ways spoke in time past to the fathers by the prophets , has in these last days spoken to us by His Son, whom He has appointed heir of all things , through whom also He made the worlds."*

3. In step 2 of AA 12 steps, "power greater of ourselves," for us as Christians we believe it is the power of the Holy Spirit, God's empowering presence who dwells in us as believers.

4. AA 12 steps is a mere integration model. It integrates Christian faith with secular model (disease model) to suit non-Christians. There is always concern regarding integrationists who are trying to combine the insights of the Scripture with a secular model. In providing such combination, the Scripture is being bent to fit nonbiblical material

that the Christians attempt to integrate with. The task of integration is impossible without ending up in a non-scriptural method.[23]

Case Study 6.1

Piers is 48-year-old. He was estranged from his family when he was young because he has learning disabilities. He started to drink alcohol at the age of 17as he had a circle of social support for drinking. He had been drinking around 8 pints of strong lager/day. He had a long forensic history of assaults, breach of peace related to drinking habit. He had a short relationship for three months with a female fellow drinker. He says she used him for money. He got two- and half-year sentence in prison after assaulting her. In prison he attended AA meetings. After prison he was admitted to dry house for 4 months and was discharged to supported accommodation. Now he has been abstinent from alcohol fore more than 3 years. He continues to attend AA meetings 3 times per week. He now has a purpose of life and feels that AA has saved his life.

Comments

This is a successful outcome for a chronic alcoholic who has managed, for more than 3 years, to be abstain from alcohol after regular attendance of AA meetings. Christians can also benefit from AA programs that are running all over the world but they need to be aware that the disease model is not a biblical route for recovery. Nouthetic counselling of Jay Adams which is based on the confrontation of sin (drinking alcohol in excess) to achieve the change or Ibrahim Youssef's model "The Mustard Seed Counselling"

---

23 Jay Adams, "Competent to Counsel: An interview with Jay Adams," *Tabletalk Magazine.* 1ˢᵗ February 2014

are biblical alternatives, as mentioned above.

Case Study 6.2

Mr Hadley saw himself as a hopeless case, a homeless, friendless, dying drunkard, who had delirium tremens (withdrawal syndrome characterised by confusion, tremors and visual hallucinations). Having found himself praying in a prison cell, he went on his release to a meeting at a Mission Hall at which Jerry M'Auley a man known for his work among drunkards, was preaching. Responding to the call at the end of the meeting, Hadley describes how, with a breaking heart, he prayed to Jesus to help him. At this a profound affective change came about: "indescribable gloom" was replaced with "glorious brightness. Hadley from that moment till now, he never wanted a drink of whiskey. He promised to God that night that if God would take the appetite for strong drink, he would work for Him all his life. God has done his part, and he have been trying to do his.[24]

Comments

This is the work of the Holy Spirit. The Lord Jesus says in John 8:36, *"therefore if the Son (the Lord Jesus) makes you free, you shall be free indeed."* The Holy Spirit dwelled in him at the moment he got saved as he was *baptised* with the Spirit. This was just the start, as he needs to walk, pray, get strength and be filled with the Spirit. He promised to serve God and he is keen to do so with the Holy Spirit's help.[25]

---

24 Cook C, C H, *Spirituality and Psychiatry*, (Royal College of Psychiatrists Publication, London. UK , 2009) page 141
25 Ibrahim Youssef, *The Mustard Seed Counselling, Author* House publication Indianapolis, IN USA (2016).

Case Study 6.3-David a Single-man Addicted to Porn[26]

Twenty-three and single, David has wrestled with pornography for years. He fights daily, some days winning, many days losing. He is doing what he should do, but he knows he needs help. So, he has come for counselling.

David's struggles started in nine grade. Several of his friends were looking at pornography on their computers, which is how he was introduced to it. He remembers looking for it on his own, and it didn't take long to find it. Started at a naked woman for the first time, he was both surprised and excited. He felt a mixture of curiosity and arousal all the same time. The day after he felt ashamed, so he avoided going back to the website for a few months. His parents hadn't said anything to him about sex, leaving him to figure it out on his own.

He lingered over that initial excited feeling, and his curiosity got to him. Two months later, he looked again. He found a pornographic site, and plunged in over the next few days, and then weeks, he looked daily, and his hunger grew, and grew. His desire for porn quickly overtook his life. One day, his father walked in as David was consuming nude pictures. Shocked, his father didn't know what to do first. Muscles on his face tightened, eyebrow furrowed, his father bellowed out, "WHAT ARE YOU DOING?" Silence. David didn't say a word. All he could do was shame. He looked down, not able to make eye contact with his father. The next thirty minutes were painful. His father cross-examined him; every question laced with anger. David owned up his struggles, but that didn't make the conversation

---

26 Case Study presented by Deepak Reju at the Biblical Counselling UK , BCUK's conference in March 2017 at the title of , *"Responding to the porn epidemic."*

any easier.

The next day, his father offered accountability. They met a couple of times over coming weeks. But, as normal, his father got busy with other things. Accountability dropped off. Left alone again, David fought his addiction on his own, and a seed of bitterness was planted in his heart.

Lord saved David at the high school through a youth group retreat. The porn stopped for a few months after his conversion. Several times he thought, "Maybe I am finally done this? But that turned out to be not true.

In college, it took no more than a few weeks before David hunted for porn again. This continued with only brief periods of reprieve. "In college I talked with my pastor, but he got frustrated with me. He kept telling me the same things-repent of my sin, read the Bible, pray, trust Christ. After a while, it was as if the pastor did not know what else to say," recalls David this time with a look of frustration, "I kept reading, repenting, and praying, but nothing changed."

After college David moved to a major city to start a new job. He resolved to do something about the problem. He read Scripture, prayed, and read books about fighting pornography, but, on his own, he didn't find success in stopping his sin.

At his first meeting with you, he confesses, "I feel like a major failure. I can go a few days without doing it, but then I always come back to it. I cannot help it. I need more. But I do it again and then I feel horrible afterwards," says David with guilt written all over his face. "It is like a dog returning to his own vomit."

David slugs his way through a stressful job. Overwhelmed by pressure, he locks the door at work and submerges himself in porn. His roommates know about the problem. Apart from you, no one else at church knows about it.

David's shame stands as a barrier that keeps him from talking to others. "I'm very embarrassed about my struggles, "he says. "I feel dirty every time I finish a bout with pornography." He talks to his best friend Jason, but transparent conversations are rare. Their schedules are so busy; they live like two ships passing in the night. David has a few friends at church, but for the most part, he feels trapped in terminally casual relationships. Most of his friendships with other men lack depth and genuine vulnerability. He feels alone,

He recently asked out a girl at the church, but she turned him down. In the aftermath, his feelings of rejection piled on top of his lingering guilt from the porn addiction.

Some days David downplays the problem. He thinks, "It is not that big of a deal," or "I can get control of it, "or "it is not going to hurt anyone," or "one day when I am married, this will all go away," or even I don't want to burden other people." At other points he obsesses over his struggle so much that he doubts whether or not he is even saved. David finally came to the end of himself and realized he was deceiving himself, which is why he came to you for help.

Doubts often plague him because his porn struggles stubbornly persist. When he describes God, he says, "I know God is good, but He is not good to me.

Deepak Reju[27] manages this case as follow:

The Four Battle Fronts[28]:

The God Front:

The focus is on the spiritual parts of this battle-anything that deals with God, Christ , sin, faith, hope etc.

We want to know about David's personal relationship with God.

David does not genuinely believe God cares about him. His distorted view of God needs to change. One thing we can do as a disciple is help David see who is-to personally understand God's character and His love.

We want to ask about David's sin struggles.

The longer an addict looks at porn, the more momentum he will have built in that direction, and the harder it will be to reverse the patterns.

Porn strugglers grow so comfortable with their sins that they lose the ferocious edge needed to win this battle. The Lord Jesus says in Mathew 5:27-28: *"You have heard that it was said to those old, "You shall not commit adultery." But I say to you that whoever looks at a woman to lust for her has already committed adultery with her in his heart."*

For Christians empowered by the Holy Spirit and the Word, only an aggressive disposition against sin is suitable for this battle.

---

27 He is a pastor of biblical counselling and family ministry at Capitol Hill Baptist Church in Washington, DC. USA. He trained at the Southern Baptist Theological Seminary where he earned his Ph.D.

28 The case management is taken from Deepak Reju's presentation of *"Responding to the Porn Epidemic,"* at the Biblical, Counselling UK , BCUK's conference, March 2017, with modification

We encourage David to pursue repentance, After repeated exposure, the distinction between good and evil also between right and wrong becomes less distinct. Also the repeated exposures to porn results in the numbed conscience. At the same time, David's carnal desires run amok. The antidote to a dulled conscience and selfish desires is a daily habit of quick repentance and consistent obedience-according to Reju.

David's consistent pattern of failure made him start accepting lies-like ha cannot change or God does not care about him. We help David by directing him to biblical passages that remind him of spiritual realities like Philippians 1:6; Romans 6:1-14.

The circumstance front:

We start by asking David to be brutal in cutting off access to pornography. A radical disposition towards his sin should lead to concrete actions. The Lord Jesus in Mathew 5:29-30 says, *"If your right eye causes you to sin, pluck it out and cast it from you; for it is more profitable for you that one of one of your members perish, than for your whole body to be cast into hell. And if your right hand causes you to sin, cut it off and cast it from you; for it is more profitable for you that one of your members perish, than for your whole body to be cast into hell."*

The self (internal)front:

David's lack of self-control can show itself not just in his behaviour, but now in his internal world, as he spends just a much time pulling images from his brain and fantasizing. Our desire is to teach the struggler to say "no to ungodliness" as in Titus 2:12 says, "teaching us that , denying ungodliness and worldly lusts, we should live soberly , righteously, and godly in the present age." Also in Philippians 4:6 says, *"Finally, brother, whatever things are true, whatever things are noble, whatever things are just, whatever things are pure, whatever things are lovely, whatever things are of good report, if there is any virtue and if there is anything praiseworthy -meditate on these things."*

The people front:

We help David connect with a person or two for accountability. Our goal is vulnerability and transparency with a close circle of friends, disciples and spiritual leaders/pastors. Biblical accountability must be honest, frequent, local and tough. Humility is a vital component in this battle as in James 4:10 says, *"Humble yourself in the sight of the Lord, and He will lift you up."*

Comments:

1. Roju ignores the spiritual warfare of Ephesians 6
2. His model has a minimal role of the Holy Spirit
3. He uses psychological terms like addiction
4. The counselling is an open-ended
5. No mention of the serious consequences of continuous sexual immorality
   - For believers: "For this reason, many of you are weak and sick and among you many sleep (die)" 1 Corinthians 11:30.
   - For unbelievers: eternal hell in the lake of brimstone and fire, "But—sexually immoral—shall have their part in the lake which burns with fire and brimstone, which is the second death." Revelation 21:8.

The Mustard Seed Counselling Model, Youssef's Model[29]:

The Early Stage of Justification:

1. Step 1: salvation: David needs to understand what is meant by salvation. Salvation is a package. After the new convert prays the sinner's prayer and accepts the Lord Jesus as his Lord and his Redeemer and Saviour, the "Mustard Seed" of faith *pistis* is implanted in his soul and been baptised with the Holy Spirit. So, he is from now on, the son of God, belongs to the believers' Church. The Holy Spirit dwells in him. Repentance is part of the package. Repentance is the change of thinking towards sin. He will develop a new desire not to grieve the Holy Spirit by watching porn. Ephesians 4:30 says, *"And do not grieve the Holy Spirit of God, by whom you were sealed for the day of redemption."*

2. Step 2: Die to the world, the flesh and the devil: Romans 6:3-4 says *"or do you know that as many of us as were baptized into Christ Jesus, were baptized into His death? Therefore, we were buried with Him through baptism into death, that just as Christ was raised from the dead by the glory of the Father., even so we also should walk in the newness of life."*

The Middle Stage of Sanctification:

3. Step 3: Faith as the key to other items of the Fruit of the Spirit of Galatians 5:22-23: here the "Mustard Seed" of faith *pistis* after been nourished by walking in the Spirit, praying and

---

29 More details from my book "the Mustard Seed Counselling," AuthorHouse publication, second edition (2020).

getting strength of the Spirit grows to produce other items of the fruit of the Spirit. The one which is the most needed in David's case is self-control over the temptation of watching porn empowered by the Holy Spirit who dwells in him as a new believer. 2 Timothy 1:7 the Apostle Paul says, *"For God has not given us a spirit of fear (in other translations, of failure), but of power and of love and of a sound mind (in other translations, self-control) ."*

4. Step 4: faith as the key to other charismatic gifts of the Spirit: here the "Mustard Seed" of faith *pistis* grows further by the filling of the Spirit to move mountains, Mathew 17:20, the Lord Jesus says, *" because of your unbelieve, for assuredly , I say to you, if you have faith as a mustard seed, you say to this mountain move from here to there and it will move and nothing will be impossible for you."* And to produce other charismatic gifts of the Spirit listed in 1 Corinthians 12:8-10.

Ephesians 5:18 says, *"And do not be drunk with wine (or other addictions), in which is dissipation, but be filled with the Spirit."* Here what is most needed is clearing (healing)of David's memory of erotic movies which reels in his imagination and the bad memories of shame and embracement as the consequences of his porn watching.

He needs also healing of his negative emotions of guilt. He needs to resist the devil, the great accuser who accuses him of his past that it might be the main reason for coming to counselling.

Another charismatic gift needed is praying in tongues where

no need for intellectual words to pray with, just get the Spirit's strength he needs to overcome temptations. In this context Ibrahim Youssef writes

A British woman, Jackie Pullinger travelled from England to Hong Kong in 1966. She had no idea that God was calling her to the Walled City-a notorious sprawling warren of slums, rates, gangsters and drug addicts in the Kowloon district. Yet as she spoke of Jesus Christ, brutal triad gangsters were converted, prostitutes left their lifestyle and Jackie discovered a new treatment for drug addiction; baptism in the Holy Spirit and speaking in tongues. Her success inspired me in formulating this Mustad Seed model which depends entirely on the fruit and the charismatic gifts of the Holy Spirit.[30]

The Final Stage of Glorification:

5. Stap 5:pull up the roots of the problem: the "Mustard Seed" of faith *pistis* prevents relapse as the root of the problem would be pulled out and implanted in the deep sea as in Luke 17:6 says, *" So the Lord said, if you have faith as a mustard seed, you can say to the mulberry tree, be pulled up by the roots and be planted in the sea and it would obey you."*

6. Stap 6: serve the Lord: as the result of the freedom from porn, David would naturally serve the Lord. One area to do this is by helping others who have such problem to be delivered from

30 Ibrahim Youssef, *The Mustard Seed Counseling*, Authorhouse publication, Bloomington IN 2nd edition 2020, page 81

this pondage, with the help and guidance of the Holy Spirit.

Chapter 7

Neuroscience

Peter Fenwick writes in his chapter in the "Spiritualty and Psychiatry" (2009)[31] that science has always been reluctant to approach spiritual matters seriously. But this attitude has changed. Spiritual medicine is defined as healing for which no known or no accepted scientific mechanism can provide an explanation.

Spiritual medicine is studied in 100% of USA medical schools now, compared to only 3% in 1995. It has been clear that the absence of spiritual values is very important factor in the genesis of illness as it is their presence in the healing of illness.

It is well known that the immune system is weakened in depression. So, no wonder the depressed person is suspectable to infection. The stress hormone cortisone, which is secreted through the adrenal-pituitary-hypothalamic pathway, is increased in depression and anxiety causing such low immunity prone to infection.

In this context, Koeng et al (1999)[32] looked at a sample of nearly 4000, 65- year-old people over 6 years period and was able to show that

31 Chris Cook et al. *Spirituality and Psychiatry*, Royal College of Psychiatrists London UK (2009). page 169-170.

32 H.G Koning et al Does religious attendance prolong survival? A six year follow up study of 3968 older adults *Journal of gerontology Medical science* 54A, M370-377

those who go to church at least once a week are more likely to be alive after 6 years. This raises important question regarding the nature of the Christian experiences of conversion, salvation, and sanctification. Such Christian practices like prayer are associated with human soul or spirit, not particularly to the body.

With the turn of the new millennium, an area of study known as neurotheology or spiritual neuroscience has emerged in the intersect between psychology, spirituality, and neuroscience:

These are examples:

1. A single photon emission computed tomography (SPECT) study demonstrated changes in cerebral activities (particularly frontal lobes, parietal lobes and left caudate) during glossolalia (speaking in tongues)[33]

2. A SPECT study measuring cerebral blood flow in Franciscan nuns in meditative prayer displayed increased activity in the prefrontal cortex and the inferior frontal and inferior parietal lobes, with changes in the prefrontal cortex reflect an altered sense of body consciousness during prayer state.

3. In 2006, functional magnetic resonance imaging (fMRI) showed brain activities in nuns while they were subjectively in state of union with God. That raise speculation concerning "God's spot" or "God region" in the brain.

Repentance/ Conversion (BEING SAVED):

---

33 CF Eugene et all, A preliminary SPECT Study, *"Psychiatry Research Neuroimaging"* 148 (2006):67-71.

Repentance or conversion (salvation)involves changes in thinking, behaving, feeling and believing. Like any change, salvation is accompanied by neurobiological changes in the brain.

Although early development of the cerebral cortex is largely genetically determined, environmental factors are keys in the new-born and continued their influence throughout an individual's life. This is particularly due to neurogenesis, which persists even in adults, but especially realized in the generation and pruning of synapses, those points of communication among cells of the brain. In this way formative influences are encoded in the synapses of the central nervous system. Hence, although our genes bias our dispositions and character, the neuronal system and pathways responsible for much of what we think, feel, believe and do are shaped by learning. Simply put in our first two years of life and beyond far more synapses are generated than are needed. Those neural connections that are used are maintained and remodelled while those that fall into disuse are eliminated.

Study was done by Guy Nave on *the Role and Function of Repentance in Luke-Acts* [34] shows that repentance in Greek is translated to *metanoia* in noun with verb *metanoeo* translated in English to "change of one's course." So, repentance is the act of change of mind, heart, view, opinion or purpose often in tandem with feelings of remorse due to the perception of having acted or thought wrongly, inappropriately or disadvantageously. *Metanoia*, if it were genuine, would be accompanied further by a will to make right the wrong committed or to change the situation that eventuated in the wrongdoing and a concomitant alternation of future behaviour. Ultimately

---

34 Guy D. Nave , *The Role and Function of Repentance in Luke-Acts,* Atlanta: Society of Biblical Literature , (2002).

metanoia would lead to forgiveness and reconciliation.

Nave emphasizes the importance of this pattern of changed thinking and living. Fundamental change in thinking that enables diverse individual to receive the salvation of God and to live together with other believers as a community of God's people.

Nave studied salvation in Luke gospel and in the book of Acts, he concludes that salvation is a process which involves two prerequisites :

1. Human response which includes *metanoia* is necessary (individuals appreciate for themselves God's offer of salvation).
2. Both *metanoia* and *metanoeo* involve change of thinking tied to change in behaviour *"fruits worthy of repentance"* (Luke 3:8) and include welcoming into the Christian community as in Acts. Accordingly, conversion is both gift and response.

However, Nave distinguishes sharply between repentance and conversion. Repentance suits Jewish population as they change there thinking towards the Lord Jesus as the Messiah who came to save them from the bondage of sins. But conversion suits the Gentile as they change their religions from worshiping idols to worshiping the living God. But his claim is not supported by the Scripture. For example, when the Apostle Paul addressed Gentile audiences in Athens, he referred to the living God and proclaimed that this God *"commands all people everywhere to repent"* (Acts 17:30).

Comments

There is no mention of the role of Holy Spirit in Nave's dissertation. The Lord Jesus says in in John 16:8, *"When He (the Holy Spirit) has come, He will convict the World of sin and righteous and of judgement."* So, the Holy

Spirit now convicts individuals of their sins to repent and direct them to the Lord Jesus as the Lamb of God who sacrificed Himself on the Cross to give forgiveness for those who believe in Him. Also, to be aware of Satan. Satan had already been judged and now is waiting to be executed and for those who follow him will share his doom. So, salvation is entirely the work of the Holy Spirit but that does not preclude the role of the individual which is to respond to the grace of God to receive[35] this precious gift of salvation as in John 3:16, *"For God so loved the world that He gave His only begotten Son, that whoever believes in Him should not perish but have everlasting life."*

Forgiveness:

Peter Fenwick (2009)[36] in his chapter of "Neuroscience of the Spirit" defines forgiveness as ceasing to feel angary or resentful towards those who hurt us. He then mentions studies that show an area of the brain called left frontal cortex used in mind judgment is showing how other people are thinking and another area in the middle temporal gyrus of the brain is activated when imagining a known person's response with another area deep in the cortex called cingulate gurus is making the forgivability judgment.

The best example in the Bible is Joseph's forgiveness. He suffered a lot from his brothers who were jealous of him and they wanted to kill him but instead they sold him as a slave. When joseph became the second man of Egypt after Pharaoh, the king of the ancient Egypt, the Bible tells us that he forgave and forgot what his brothers had done for him. When he had

---

35 In the sense that they do not need to do good deeds to receive this gift.
36 Peter Fenwick, *Neuroscience of the Spirit*, Spirituality and Psychiatry, Royal College of Psychiatrists, London UK (2009)pages 174-175

his first born son, he named him *"Manasseh"* as he said , *"For God has made me forget all my toil and all my father's house."* (Genesis 41:51). To note that Joseph did not resume the relationship with his brothers until they repented and changed.

Spiritual healing:

Fenwick (2009)[37] examines literature of spiritual healing that been practiced by shamanic[38] practice and found healing in this practice. For example, the relief of pain with functional improvement for those who suffer from temporo-mandibular disorder.

However, this is nothing compared to the gift of healings for those who are filled with the Holy Spirit and have such gift from the Spirit as recorded in 1Cornithians 12:9, *"to another gifts of healings by the same Spirit."* More details about this gift are in my book, "The Mustard Seed Counselling."[39]

In this context R.T. Kendall[40] recalls Oral Roberts[41] as he visited him at his home three times. During the years of 1952-1954, he had seen extraordinary healings. but not afterwards which means the gift of healings

---

37 The same reference above pages 181-182.

38 People in northern Asia and North America who believe that they are able to contact good and evil spirits, Oxford English dictionary page 768.

39 Ibrahim Youssef, *The Mustard Seed Counselling,* AuthorHouse publication, Bloomington IN, 2nd edition (2020)

40 R.T Kendall, *Holy Fire*, Lake Mary, Florida: Charismata House (2014) pp 145-151

41 The reader can go to "YouTube" and see some of these wonderful healings

can come and go.

Miracles:

Fenwick defines miracles as an act of healing attributed to the intervention of God without a clear physical mechanism to bring the change. Fenwick then goes on to describe a couple of miracles that were done by St Thomas and St Cuthbert and concludes that we have all been so conditioned by scientific methods that we either no longer allow miracles to occur or are blind to those that do.

Again, nothing compares with the gift of miracles that is given by the Holy Spirit to believers who are filled with the Spirit as in 1Corithians 12:10, *"to another the workings of miracles—"* More details are in my book "The Mustard Seed Counselling".

Case Study 7.1

John 11:33-43: *Therefore, when Jesus saw her (Mary, Lazarus's sister) weeping and the Jews who came with her weeping, He groaned in the spirit and was troubled. And He said, "where have you laid him?" They said to Him, "Lord, come and see.". Jesus wept. Then the Jews said, "See how He loved him!" And some of them said, "Could not this man who opened the eyes of the blind, also have kept this man from dying?"" Then Jesus again groaning in Himself came to the tomb. It was a cave and stone lay against it. Jesus said, "take away the stone. Martha the (other) sister of him who was dead, said to Him, "Lord by this time there is a stench, for he has been dead four days. Jesus said to Her, "Did I not say to you that if you would believe you would see the glory of the God?" Then they took away the stone from the place where the dead man was lying. And Jesus lifted up his eye and said, "Father, I thank You that you have heard*

Me. And I know that You always hear Me, but because of the people who are standing by I said this that they may believe that You sent Me." Now when He had said these things, He cried with a loud voice, "Lazarus, come forth!" And he who had died, came out bound hand and foot with grave clothes, and his face was wrapped with a cloth. Jesus said to them, "Loose him and let him go."

Comments

This case study shows that the Lord Jesus when he was on earth was God manifested in flesh as He raised Lazarus from the dead after he was a stench and been in the tomb for 4 days, and full man as He groaned in the spirit, troubled, wept etc.

Chapter 8
The Resurrection of the Body

I devote this chapter in my book as I find an urging need to convince the readers, from the Scripture, that there is life after death. From my experience in psychiatry, individuals who attempt suicide, they say there is no life after death. Death for them is the end of all things. So, for them there is nothing to worry about. Albeit the psychiatrists try to convince such individuals to think of their families and friends. They need to think of them. From this angle, the psychiatrists try to convince them not to kill themselves, nothing more.

From biblical perspective, the Lord Jesus said to Martha when her brother Lazarus died and been in the tomb for 4 days so the body was a stench, *"I am the resurrection and the life. He who believes in Me, though he may die, he shall live. And whoever lives and believes in Me shall never die. Do you believe this?"* (John 11:25-26).

The Christian believers believe in the resurrection of the bodies and what is impossible for man is possible for God. But still some questions needed to be answered. <u>First,</u> would it be possible to reconstitute the body of one individual without violating the integrity of other bodies? <u>Second</u>, how can I be sure that it is me that enjoys eternal life is really me? Here we raise the question of personal embodied in resurrection and the possibility of survival of the personal identity in particular. This suggests a dualist anthropology, mortal body, immortal soul. This also raises the possibility of three-stage progression: death, followed by a temporary state of disembodied existence followed by the resurrection and judgment in the last day.

The Intermediate State:

The intermediate state is defined as the period of time that elapsed from the individual's death to the resurrection of the dead. According to the book of revelation there will be two kinds of resurrections. The resurrection of the believers in the second coming of the Lord Jesus when the dead in Christ will raise first and for us who are still alive (I hope) will follow. For us, as believers, we will stand before the Christ's seat where we get rewards every one according to his/her good deeds -1 Thessalonians 4:13-18, the Apostle Paul says : *"But do not want you to be ignorant, brethren, concerning those who have fallen asleep(died)lest you sorrow as others who have no hope. For if we believe that Jesus died and rose again, even so God will bring with Him those who sleep in Jesus. For this we say to you by the word of the Lord, that we who are alive and remain until the coming of the Lord will by no means precede those who are asleep. For the Lord Himself will descend from heaven with a shout with the voice of an archangel, and with the trumpet of God. And the dead in Christ will rise first. Then we who are alive and remain shall be caught up together with them in the clouds to meet the Lord in the air. And thus, we shall always be with the Lord. Therefore comfort one another with these words."*

For the unbelievers, there will be another resurrection for judgement which will be after the Christ's second coming, the 7 years of tribulation and great tribulation, and the millennium when the Lord resigns for 1000 years, as the book of revelation confirms.

Joel B. Green (2008)[42] examines this intermediate state according to two passages of the Scripture: The parable of the rich man and Lazarus (Luke 16:19-31 and Jesus and the criminal at the crucifixion (Luke 23:40-43).

The parable of the rich man and Lazarus (Luke 16:19-31):

The Lord Jesus in this parable mentions an unnamed rich man appears in Hades (sheol in Hebrew means question mark "?"as there is no text explains the after death in the Old Testament),and Lazarus in Abraham's bosom. Thus, while Lazarus is in a blissful state, the wealthy man experiences torment in Hades. So, the righteous already is participating in rewards, while the wicked already is suffering punishment. Here also we notice that personal identity is obvious and what it made it intermediate state is that the rich man's brothers are still alive in earth.

However, the human agents in corporeal experiences are persevered like thirst, speak, and presumably fetch water. So, it is not a soul or spirit that manifests such things. That makes the story of the Lord Jesus is likely to be a parable.

The Lord Jesus and the criminal at the crucifixion (Luke 23:40-43):

Luke alone records the exchange between the two criminals and the Lord Jesus at the scene of their crucifixion. The first criminal blasphemes the Lord while at the same time identifying himself with Lord (save yourself and us!), whereas the second demonstrates insight into the Lord's identity and status as God's agent of salvation as obvious in his plea *"Remember me!"* He spoke to Yahweh whose memory is a source of divine blessing in

---

42 Joel B. Green, *Body , Soul and Human Life,* Baker Academic , Grand Rapids, Michigan (2008) pp157-166.

keeping with His covenant. Of particular interest here is the Lord's reply *"Truly I tell you, today you will be with me in paradise."* Here Luke emphasis is on two things: the immediacy of salvation and the intermediate resting place of the soul in paradise, where the Lord's human-soul stayed there for three days before resurrection.

The Disciples and the Resurrected Jesus (Luke 24:36-49):

Our concern with the nature of life after the grave and continuity of personal identity from life after death is highlighted by the resurrected Lord Jesus. The Lord's human-soul passed the intermediate state in paradise and was raised in a glorified body. In this glorified body we find evidence that Jesus' post-resurrection bodily existence was out of ordinary. For example, He entered the upper room with the doors locked, and His personal identity persevered as the Lord Jesus told the disciples," *Be hold My hands and My feet. That it is Myself. Handle Me and see, for a spirit does not have flesh and bones as you see I have."* (Luke 39:24).

So, the Lord Jesus showed the disciples it was Him. <u>First,</u> the disciples did not mistake him (persevered His personal identity). <u>Second,</u> Jesus presented to the disciples as a fully embodied (flesh and bones) person. <u>Third</u> in Luke 24:44 When the Lord appeared to the two disciples on the route of Emmaus, *"He then said to them , "these are the words which I spoke to you while I was still with you, that all things must be fulfilled which were written in the Law of Moses and the Prophets and the Psalms concerning Me,"*

Joel Green concludes[43]:

---

43 Joel Green, *Body, Soul, and Human Life* pp 169,170

"Resurrection is not soul flight, but the exclamation point and essential affirmation that Jesus has place on display for all to see a life of service, even the service of life-giving death and that this life carries with it the divine imprimatur, actualizing as it does God's own redemptive project."

The Resurrection Body in the first and second Corinthians

The passage of 2 Corinthians 5:1-10 provides the most pressing evidence in Paul for a body-soul dualism in an intermediate state especially verses 1:3, *"For we know that if our earthly house, this tent is destroyed, we have a building from God a house not made with hands, eternal in the heavens. For in this we groan, earnestly desiring to be clothed with our habitation which is from heaven, if indeed, having been clothed, we should not be found naked."* So, at death the soul is freed in an intermediate state which is not in a desirable state (naked) waiting for the resurrection in a glorified body for the believers. So, in this intermediate state the soul is bodiless(naked).

In 1 Corinthians 15, Paul defends belief in the future resurrection as the denial of the future resurrection is a denial of the resurrection of Christ, as the "first fruit." Therefore, in order for Christian believers to share eternal life, their bodies must be transformed for the new conditions of life with God forever. In Genesis, Adam had such a body, but rather subject to death and decay on account of sin and therefore was ill-suited for eternal life with God. The first man, Adam, became a living being. However, the last Adam, Christ, became a life -giving spirit. The first Adam was dusty, the second Adam, in Christ, is heavenly. *"So also, is the resurrection of the dead. The body is sown in corruption, it is raised in no corruption. It is sown in dishonour; it is raised in glory. It is sown in weakness; it is raised in power. there is sown a natural body, and there is a spiritual body."* (1 Corinthians 15:42-44). So, the resurrection and embodied afterlife are God's doing, a divine gift.

Bibliography

Adams, E Jay. Competent to Counsel: An Interview with Jay Adams, " *TableTalk Magazine* February 1ˢᵗ, 2014.

Alcoholic Anonymous, World Service in 1999, *Twelve Steps and Twelve Traditions,* New York, 1999.

American Psychiatric Association, *DSM-IV-TR*. Arlington, VA, 2000. Cook, C.H, *Alcohol Addiction* and *Christian Ethics*. Cambridge University Press, 2006.

Cook, C.H.et al. Spirituality and Psychiatry. Royal College Publication London UK,2009.

Eugene et al, A Preliminary SPECT Study, *"Psychiatry Research Neuroimaging."* 2006.

Freud. S. T*he Future of an Illusion. In the Complete Works of Sigmoid Freu,* d Hogan Press, 1927.

Green B. Joel, *Body, Soul, and Human Life, The Mature of Humanity in the Bible*, The Bakar Academic, Grand Rapids, MI 2008.

Holy Bible. New King James Version. Thomas Nelson, Inc 1982.

Jardine Samuel, The Person and Work of the Holy Spirit. Stanton Drew, Bristol: Seed Publication 2010.

Kendall. R.T. *Totally Forgiving Ourselves*, Hodder &Stoughton. London. UK, 2007.

Koenig, Michael et al. "Damage to the Prefrontal Cortex Increases Utilitarian Moral Judgement", *Nature*. March 2007.

Nave Jr., Guy D. *The Role and Function of Repentance in Luke-Acts*, SBLAB 4. Atlanta: Society of Biblical Literature, 2002.

Reju Deepak, *Responding to the Porn Epidemic*, Biblical Counselling UK conference Derbyshire UK March 2017.

Williams Chris et al, *I am Not Supposed to Feel Like This*. Hodder &Stoughton. London. UK, 2002.

Youssef Ibrahim, *"The Mustard Seed Counseling"* AuthorhHouse publication, Bloomington IN 2nd ed. 2020.

www.ingramcontent.com/pod-product-compliance
Lightning Source LLC
Chambersburg PA
CBHW051552120626
46551CB00013B/1478